Golf Trivia Quiz Book

Bill Kroen

BARNES
&NOBLE
BOOKS
NEW YORK

To Mark Coady who loved golf and life.

ISBN 0-7607-3069-5

Book design by Lundquist Design, New York

Printed and bound in the United States of America

02 03 MP 9 8 7 6 5 4 3 2 1

OPM

The Game

Q: What did Mark Twain have to say about golf?

Q: Why is golf so named?

Q: Why are sand traps called "bunkers"?

A: He called it "a good walk spoiled."

A: The word "golf" comes from the German word *kolbe,* which means club. The name has been used for many games played with clubs (the Dutch game *kolven,* for example). A debate about the origin of golf has been ongoing: Did it begin with the Flemish game of *chole,* the French *jeu de mail,* or the Roman game of *Paganica* (the game of countrymen)? No one knows. The Scots, however, were the first to play the game of golf as it is played today. The first recorded reference to golf came in an Act of Scottish Parliament in 1457 that forbade golf and "futeball" because Scotland was at war with England, and the government didn't want young men neglecting military training.

A: "Bunker" comes from the Scottish *bonker,* meaning a chest or box where coal is kept, usually dug into the side of a hill. Often, cows would graze in the marshlands adjacent to the old links courses, standing alongside the dunes and creating a depression that reminded Scottish players of these chests, and eventually these areas became known as bunkers.

Q: Why is the word "bogey" used to describe a score of one over par?

Q: Why is the word "birdie" used for a score of one under par on a hole?

Q: Why are the spectators at a golf tournament called a "gallery"?

Q: Why is the Masters considered one of the Grand Slam tournaments?

A: The term comes from an imaginary Colonel Bogey of the
      Great Yarmouth Club in England. It is believed that a
      Major Charles Wellman, while playing against ground
      score (par), referred to failing to get par as "getting caught
      by the bogey man," a phrase from a popular eighteenth-
      century tune. The members of the club began referring to
      an imaginary new member, Colonel Bogey, who would
      always shoot even par. As the game spread to the United
      States, "bogey" was narrowed to represent a score of one
      over par on a hole.

A: According to *Golf Magazine*'s *Encyclopedia of Golf*, "birdie"
      was coined in the United States. In 1903 a certain A. H.
      Smith of Atlantic City is said to have remarked after holing
      out, "That's a bird of a shot!" The words "eagle" and "double
      eagle" are outgrowths of the bird reference.

A: In British theaters the large balcony containing the cheaper
      seats is called a gallery. Over the years the term has come to
      signify the public in general.

A: The Masters is the only privately run tournament of the big
      four considered to be the Grand Slam of golf. The U.S.
      Open, the PGA Championship and the British Open are
      all run and sanctioned by national golf institutions. The
      Masters has attained its prestigious place in golf history and
      lore with a great course, excellent ambience, exclusiveness,
      tradition and careful promotion. Bobby Jones started the
      Masters in 1934 as a starting tournament for the pro tour as
      the pros headed north after the winter season in Florida.

Q: Why are some tournaments called "opens"?

Q: Why and how is par assigned to a hole?

Q: Why is four the accepted number of golfers for one group?

Q: Why is it considered bad form to walk across someone's line before he or she putts?

A: "Open" means that the tournament is open to both amateurs and professionals.

A: Par is the score that an expert golfer should make on that particular hole; it is set in order to have a standard against which to measure score and determine handicaps. Par is generally based on the length of the hole, but allowances are made for level of difficulty caused by terrain features. The USGA's guidelines for par according to distance are:

Par	Men	Women
3	up to 250	up to 210
4	251 to 470	211 to 400
5	over 470	401 to 575

A: In its earliest form, golf was strictly match play in format, and four is the smallest number of players for team matches. As a result, competition between clubs in England and America in the nineteenth century was always in the foursome grouping. Even as the format changed, however, numbers greater than four were generally frowned upon because they slowed down the game and caused confusion around the green.

A: There are two main reasons why this breach of etiquette is considered serious. Firstly, by walking on someone's line, you may leave an indentation that could affect the roll of the putt. Secondly, the intrusion across a player's line may cause a break in the player's concentration.

Q: In the early days of golf, why were feathers used as stuffing for golf balls?

Q: Why is a game of golf referred to as a "round"?

Q: Why is the word "divot" used to describe a piece of earth dislodged by a club stroke?

Q: Why is the tradition of "having the honor"— allowing the player who scored the lowest on the previous hole to tee off first—used, and what, if any, advantage does it bestow?

Q: Why is the overlapping grip sometimes called the "Vardon"?

A: The old "featheries" were surprisingly alive. A large amount of chicken feathers was boiled and then stuffed firmly into a leather cover. When the feathers dried and expanded they stretched the leather so it became quite resilient. The ball actually went a good distance, with drives of over 300 yards recorded, but the ball was phased out about 1850.

A: In the early days of golf, all courses were constructed in a circular fashion. The first hole was near the clubhouse, and the other holes would circle through the countryside, coming back to the starting point on the eighteenth hole.

A: "Divot" is a Scottish word for a piece of turf.

A: Having the honor is part of the rules, establishing a uniform system of order for playing first off the tee. To hit first can be a distinct advantage, as a good shot may put pressure on an opponent.

A: Harry Vardon, who won the British Open six times and the U.S. Open once, was a great promoter and golfer at the turn of the century. He was often photographed using the overlap grip. He is not, however, considered to be the inventor of the grip, as several well-known players, including Leslie Balfour Melville and J. H. Taylor, had used the grip successfully before Vardon reached fame as a golfer.

Q: Why is the higher side of a cup on an incline called "the pro side"?

Q: Why are golf courses sometimes called "links"?

Q: Why is "nassau" used to describe a match played on both nines and an overall eighteen?

Q: Why is the term "dormie" used when someone is ahead by the same number of holes left in the match?

Q: Why is the word "putt" used in golf?

A: A good player will read the break of a putt correctly, allowing enough break and putting to the higher side. The lower side of the hole is sometimes called "the sucker's side" because the poor golfer will not read the break correctly.

A: According to Webster Evans's *Encyclopedia of Golf* the word is derived from Old English *hlinc,* meaning ridge of land. Links land is gently undulating land, often running along the seashore. In the strict sense of the term, a links golf course should be one that borders the sea.

A: A nassau bet sets up three separate matches: the front nine, the back nine and the entire eighteen holes. When a player or side goes down by two holes, a "press" can be made. A press doubles the amount of the bet and creates a new match for the number of holes remaining. This popular form of match comes from a betting practice that was very popular in the Caribbean Islands. The practice spread to the United States.

A: "Dormie" probably comes from the Latin *dormire* "to sleep." "The player who is ahead cannot lose though he go to sleep."

A: Putt comes from the word "put." Once on the green, the object of that particular stroke is to "put" the ball into the hole.

Q: Why is the Ryder Cup match so named?

Q: Why is the term "bye" used when a player does not have an opponent in a match?

Q: Why does "fairway" describe the close-cut part of a course?

Q: Why is the term "mulligan" used for the granting of a second chance at a drive on the first hole?

Q: Why is a very poor round of golf sometimes referred to as "military golf"?

Q: Why is a "skins" competition so named?

A: The Ryder Cup matches are played between American PGA professionals and European pros every two years. An unofficial match between the U.S. and England played in Surrey, England, in 1926 prompted the tradition; the match was very popular and a wealthy seed merchant named Samuel Ryder presented a gold cup at the first official match at Worcester, Massachusetts, in 1927, with the American team winning.

A: The term "bye" probably started as a farewell to someone who had lost a match 10 and 8 in an eighteen-hole match. Not having to play the remaining holes, an opponent in this situation also had a "bye," and gradually the term was extended to anyone who did not have to play a match.

A: The Rules of Golf do not specifically define the word "fairway" but generally refer to it as "through the green." In early references to the game, the playing area was often called the "fair green." As time went on, the term "fairway," as opposed to the "rough," became most common.

A: The origin of "mulligan" is not clear, but it may be rhyming slang for "have at it again."

A: A hacker having an extremely wild day off the tee calls to mind a drill sergeant's cadence call: "Left-right-left-right!"

A: In a "skins" game players compete on each hole, the player with the lowest score winning a "skin." The term goes back to the days when a hunter would display his success by the number of pelts or skins he had upon returning from the hunt.

Q: Why is the phrase "rub of the green" used to describe any odd or accidental occurrence in the game of golf?

Q: Why is the word "stymie" used in golf?

Q: Why do golfers tend to dress in very colorful attire?

Q: Why do many instructional books equate an "average" golfer with a poor one?

A: The 1812 code of the Royal and Ancient Golf Committee used the following expression in Rule IX: "Whatever happens to a ball by accident must be reckoned a rub of the green." "Rub" here means a hindrance or difficulty, and "green" is a common term for the whole course.

A: The word "stymie" comes from the Scottish word *styme*, meaning a person who is partially blind. In golf, stymie rules used to allow a golfer to putt his ball onto the line of his opponent in order to block the path to the hole. If you were stymied, you could not "see" the hole. Stymies were taken out of the Rules in 1952 as they tended to lessen the importance of true golfing skill and slow the game down. Today, "stymied" is used by golfers to describe a situation where they are blocked along their line to the green by an obstacle such as a tree or large rock.

A: The tradition of bright clothing goes back to the very beginnings of the game. Archers would wear bright red uniforms for much the same reason hunters wear orange and red today. As the early clubs were often made up of mostly military men, the idea of wearing bright clothing in order to be seen while playing carried over to the game of golf.

A: Golf is a very difficult game to master. According to the National Golf Foundation, the average golfer will shoot in the high 90s on a par 72 course. Only one player in twelve will break eighty with any consistency. The practice, experience, knowledge and athletic ability needed to play golf is well beyond the level possible for the "average" golfer.

Q: Why is the term "Grand Slam" used to describe winning the U.S. Open, British Open, PGA Championship and the Masters?

Q: Why is three under par on one hole sometimes referred to as an "albatross"?

Q: Why is the handicap system often used at amateur net tournaments called the "Callaway System"?

Q: Why is the Walker Cup so named?

A: "Grand Slam," with its baseball meaning obviously in mind, was first used in golf to describe Bobby Jones's amazing feat in 1930 of winning the U.S. and British Opens and the national amateur championships of both countries. With the lessening in importance of amateur play, the phrase eventually arrived at its modern meaning.

A: "Albatross" is simply an extension of birdie and eagle and like them is considered an American term. The word never really caught on among golfers, however, and the term "double eagle" has generally replaced it in modern golf vernacular.

A: In 1957 Lionel F. Callaway invented a system that yields instant handicaps based on the round shot. The system is used extensively when large numbers of competitors who do not have handicaps play. The system eliminates the worst score of the round in descending order based on the total score for the day.

A: The Walker Cup matches are played between the top amateurs from the United States and Great Britain. The Cup began with an unofficial match the day before the British Amateur Championship in 1921. George H. Walker, president of the United States Golf Association, had agreed to provide a cup for the winning team starting in 1922. The newspapers quickly referred to it as the Walker Cup and the name stuck.

Q: Why is the Curtis Cup so named?

Q: Why do golfers yell "fore!" to warn others of an approaching shot?

Q: Why are there eighteen holes on a golf course?

A: The Curtis Cup matches are played between the top
     women amateurs from the United States and Great Britain
     every two years. An unofficial competition, begun in 1905
     between the two countries, steadily grew in popularity until
     it was decided to begin an official event in 1932. Two
     sisters, Margaret and Harriet Curtis, had played in many of
     the unofficial matches and offered to donate a cup for the
     competition. The Curtis sisters had won four USGA
     Ladies' Championships between them at the time.

A: Most experts think the term derives from a warning used
     by the British Army in battle, which formed ranks of
     infantry at the front with artillery located to the rear. Before
     firing a volley, the artillery yelled "beware before" to the
     infantry, who then lay down to let the cannonballs fly
     overhead. Shortened to "fore," the term eventually came to
     be used by golfers to warn other players of a missile headed
     their way.

A: The number of holes on a golf course was not fixed until
     the eighteenth century. In 1764 the Royal and Ancient
     Golf Club reduced its number of holes from twenty-two to
     eighteen by combining eight of them into four. As
     legislation on the Rules was being written at the same time,
     eighteen was agreed upon by common consent.

Q: Why is the term "caddy" used in golf, and what is its history?

Q: Why is stroke play called "medal play"?

Q: Why are hollows or small streams on Scotland's courses called "burns"?

Q: Why is the name "Stableford" given to a point scoring system that is used on one PGA Tour event?

A: The word probably comes from the French word *cadet*, meaning "young man." Mary Queen of Scots, an avid golfer, used the young men of her court to carry her clubs. The word had been adopted by the Scottish to refer to a porter or someone who does odd jobs, but partly because of Mary's use "caddy" was gradually applied to the young men who did the various jobs as greenskeeper, club repairer and ballmarker around the course before narrowing in meaning to its present use.

A: In the early days of golf in England and Scotland, there were no trophies given to the winners of club championships. Instead, a medal was given to the winner, and he was bestowed with the title of "Captain" for one year. The medals are now considered very valuable among golf collectors.

A: The small streams that run across and through the courses of Scotland become water hazards. It was said that players who hit their balls into them "got burned" by them.

A: The name comes from The Stableford Club in Yorkshire, England, where it is alleged to have been started by its members. In Stableford scoring, five points are awarded for an eagle, three for a birdie, and one for a par. Subtractions are made for scores over par. The PGA Tour plays a modified version of the Stableford.

The Equipment

Q: Why does a golf ball have dimples?

Q: Why does a golf club have grooves?

Q: Why do some putters have grips that are flat on the top?

Q: Why are wood clubs rounded on the face instead of flat from heel to toe?

A: The primary function of dimples is to provide lift. As the ball spins off the club, the tiny cups trap air in such a way that the air moves more quickly over the top of the ball than around the bottom, causing the ball to rise. This aerodynamic principle is the same as the one that causes airplanes to lift off the ground.

A: The grooves on a club stop the ball from sliding up the clubface at impact. As a ball is struck, it will ride up on the clubface until the grooves and dimples of the ball interact to trap the ball and help propel it forward. The grooves also create backspin which allows the ball to take flight.

A: Under the Rules of Golf (4-1c), putters are the only clubs that can have such grips. The purpose of the flat grip is to accommodate the most common putting grip, which places both thumbs directly down the middle of the shaft. This grip helps prevent the hands from rolling and thus throwing the ball off line.

A: This feature is called "bulge." The slight curve from heel to toe actually helps shots that are mis-hit. A ball struck on the toe, for example, will fly off to the right, but the bulge on the clubface will give it a counterclockwise spin, causing it to hook back toward the center of the fairway. A ball struck on the heel will react in the opposite manner.

Q: Why are the spikes on golf shoes so arranged?

Q: Why aren't golf balls numbered higher—such as 9, 10 or 11?

Q: Why are some new clubs featuring "offset" as a game-improvement aid?

A: The proper golf swing requires that a golfer maintain good balance while shifting weight from one foot to the other. The spikes on most golf shoes are placed so that they line the outsides of both the heel and sole areas. This design allows the golfer to push off the back foot on the downswing, with his front foot receiving the weight transfer without slipping forward at impact and beyond.

A: In the late fifties and early sixties, several golf ball manufacturers did number balls into the double figures. Touring pros, out of superstition, tended to only use low-numbered balls, those numbered 1 through 3 in particular. The everyday golfer soon picked up on the practice and the manufacturers adjusted accordingly.

A: An offset club is one in which the clubface is set back from the hosel, a design feature that allows the golfer to set up for the shot with his hands in front of the ball and promotes a swing that hits down on the ball. Offset woods help the player eliminate slices as well.

Q: Why is a sand wedge designed differently from other clubs?

Q: Why did wood clubs have tightly wound string around the neck of the club?

Q: Why are some clubs curved on the bottom and advertised as "radiused"?

A: A sand wedge is specifically designed to slide under the ball through the sand. The back of the flange or bottom of the club is lower than the front or lead edge of the club. This design feature, called "bounce," allows the club to pass through the sand without becoming buried. In a sand shot, the clubface never actually touches the ball; the concussion of the club striking the sand actually causes the ball to fly up and out of the trap.

A: Called "whipping," the tightly wound twine served to reinforce the joint where the shaft meets the clubhead. Without this reinforcement the wood near the neck would crack and split from the force of the swing. Today, various materials are used instead of whipping to reinforce the joint.

A: "Radiused," "cambered" or "rocker-soled" clubs are curved from heel to toe to enable the average golfer to make more solid contact from various lies. With a curved sole, only a small part of the leading edge of the club comes into contact with the turf. A radiused club is particularly advantageous for lies on hard pan, or where fairways are dry and grass is sparse.

Q: Why are some wood clubs said to be "persimmon"?

Q: Why have some manufacturers started using titanium in their shafts?

Q: Why are golf grips tapered from top to bottom when the grips of tennis rackets, fishing rods and baseball bats, for example, are either straight or tapered upwards?

Q: Why are manufacturers using metal in the construction of "woods"?

A: Persimmon is a term used for trees that belong to the ebony family, which have fine, hard wood. In golf, a persimmon wood is one that is made from a solid block of wood. In contrast, a wood club made from gluing layers of wood together is called "laminated." Metal woods are sometimes referred to as "Pittsburgh Persimmon."

A: Titanium, famous for its use in aircrafts, is lighter than steel and has excellent properties of flex and torque. The lightness of titanium shafts creates a lower center of gravity. Because of this shift in weight, the club can be swung easily and still generate good clubhead speed because the new weighting characteristic keeps the "kick" in the shaft.

A: There are several reasons for the shape of the golf grip. Firstly, the shaft of a golf club must taper from top to bottom to flex properly for the golf swing. Also, the golf grip places the two hands closely together so that the meat of the hands is at the top and the fingers at the bottom. Finally, the tapering of the grip allows greater freedom of wrist action, vital to the proper golf swing.

A: The metal woods offer the opportunity to create different weight characteristics that can help a golf game. Perimeter weighting, for example, placing weight around the perimeter of the clubface, reduces the amount of twisting at impact. This feature, theoretically, should cause off-center hits to fly straighter.

Q: Why is the word "tee" used for the wooden peg that holds the ball?

Q: Why are the clubfaces of woods rounded from top to bottom?

Q: Why were the earlier models of golf balls called "gutta-percha"?

Q: Why are some clubs featuring "cavity back" designs?

A: The word "tee" probably comes from the Scottish *teay*, a small pile of sand. For many years golfers would make a pile of sand or dirt and place their ball on top of it for driving. In 1920 Dr. William Lowell, a Boston dentist, invented the wooden tee to prevent his hands from becoming scratched.

A: It is mostly a matter of appearance and optics. The clubface is rounded from top to bottom to give the appearance of loft. If the face were cut straight from top to bottom, it would appear almost vertical to the golfer. By rounding, or creating "roll," golf manufacturers are actually helping golfers' confidence in getting the ball into the air.

A: *Gutta-percha* is a material tapped from several species of Malaysian trees. It resembles rubber but contains more resin and hardens when exposed to air. Golf legend has it that a professor at St. Andrews University received a statue of Vishnu packed in *gutta-percha*. An avid golfer, the professor rolled the material and tried it out as a golf ball.

A: "Cavity back" clubs are usually investment clubs with a hollowed-out area directly behind the hitting area. This design feature allows club-makers to place additional weight in the heel and toe areas and consequently help the golfer hit straighter shots from off-center hits.

Q: Why do some club manufacturers refer to a "moment of inertia" in describing the characteristics of their clubs?

Q: Why do many golf ball companies feature such numbers as 382 and 384 on their balls?

Q: Why do golf balls have compression ratings of 80, 90, and 100?

Q: Why are tees still made of wood instead of more durable materials?

A: The moment of inertia is the measure of any object's inertial resistance to turning. The moment of inertia is related to weight and the distribution of weight of the object to be turned. In the clubface, a perimeter weighting or heel-toe weighting design will help prevent twisting by increasing the moment of inertia when shots are hit slightly off of the sweet spot.

A: The numbers refer to the number of dimples on the ball. The dimples are arranged in certain patterns to produce desired flight characteristics. For example, Maxfli's DDH design is an arrangement of dimples in a dodecahedron pattern that promotes lift and carry in a stabilized flight.

A: The compression ratings of 80 (soft), 90 (medium), and 100 (hard) measure the technical concept of "coefficient or restitution," which refers to a ball's ability to spring back into shape after being struck. Tests have shown that the higher the compression the farther the ball will go, regardless of the force of the swing. The soft and medium compression balls are favored by many players because they offer a better feel.

A: Tees have been made of wood for over sixty years for several reasons. Firstly, tees made of metal and plastic can scratch and damage wood clubs. The cost of wooden tees has remained very low, and the supply is plentiful. Of course, as with most things in the game of golf, there is tradition. Many top players would never dream of playing with anything but a wooden tee, and the vast majority use white ones only.

Q: Why were aluminum shafts phased out?

Q: Why is the USGA's robot used for testing golf balls and clubs called "Iron Byron"?

Q: Why were the knickers that golfers used to wear called "plus fours"?

Q: Why are Ping clubs so named?

A: Aluminum proved to be too soft for golf shafts, unable to take the tremendous torque and flex involved in the golf swing. Players using aluminum in the late sixties found that the sound at impact was muffled and the distance off the tee quite reduced.

A: Iron Byron was actually modeled after the swing of Byron Nelson. The USGA wanted a robot that would replicate a near-perfect golf swing based on the swing plane, arc, and height of an average-sized man. Nelson's swing, considered to be a classic example of the proper golf swing, was used to set the baseline data for the robot to emulate.

A: In order to create the effect of pants bloused just below the knee, manufacturers added four inches to the normal length of short pants. Thus the length of the knickers was normal length plus four inches.

A: Karsten Solheim, founder of Ping clubs and Karsten Manufacturing, made his first putter on his workbench. The putter was intended to be lightweight and feature heel-and toe-weighing. When Solheim tried it for the first time he was surprised to hear a rather pronounced ping! when he struck the putt. Thus the Ping was born.

Q: Why is the grain in persimmon woods important?

Q: Why was there once a difference between the size of golf balls used in Great Britain and the U.S.?

Q: Why do grips come in different thicknesses?

Q: Why and how is a "Stimpmeter" used in golf?

A: Most golf-club mavens look for a matching grain pattern
     through all the wood clubs as a sign of careful
     craftsmanship and matching stocks of wood.

A: The difference in size (U.S. 1.68 inches; G.B. 1.62) goes
     back to 1931, when the USGA approved the 1.68 diameter
     as the standard for golf competition. The Royal and
     Ancient Golf Committee did not go along with the change,
     and the two countries played with different-sized balls. In
     1990, however, the ball was standardized at 1.68
     throughout the world.

A: The grip differences come in increments of 1/32 of an inch
     and may have an effect on the swing. Thicker grips tend to
     restrict wrist and hand action and can help to prevent
     hooking. On the other hand, thinner grips promote greater
     hand and wrist action and can help cure a slice.

A: A Stimpmeter is a grooved bar used to measure the speed
     of greens. A ball is placed on the bar, which is raised until
     the ball rolls freely. The distance that the ball rolls is
     measured and the operation is repeated several times, with
     an average being taken. The speed of a green is important
     to ensure consistency and to create conditions that are
     considered to be of championship caliber.

Q: Why do some manufacturers use beryllium copper on clubheads?

Q: Why is a putter used from off the green called a "Texas wedge"?

Q: Why do shafts come in different flexes?

A: Beryllium copper adds weight to the clubhead, cuts down on glare and allows the grooves to be cut more sharply into the clubface.

A: Many players from Texas used this technique because of the tough wind conditions there. Using a putter keeps the shots low and the wind's influence minimal. Ben Hogan popularized the technique and the term in the 1950s.

A: Most club manufacturers make four flexes for their shafts. Generally, the type of flex depends on the amount of force exerted on the swing. A powerful swing requires a shaft with little flex in it, as the force of the swing would cause a whippy shaft to bend too much so that the clubhead would strike the ball too soon in the player's swing. Additionally, the clubhead would twist as it reached impact, causing a severe hook. On the other hand, a player who swings easily needs a more flexible shaft in order to have some "kick" or benefit from the shaft bending as a result of centrifugal force. The four standard flexes are:

X-Stiff — Very powerful swing
Stiff — Strong player
Regular — Normal swing, average player
Soft — Very slow swing

Q: Why are some irons referred to as "muscle back"?

Q: Why is the word "Modulus" used on graphite shafts?

Q: Why did early putters have quite an amount of loft?

Q: Why are some manufacturers using titanium in their golf balls?

Q: Why are titanium irons so large?

A: The term "muscle back" refers to forged irons that have bulges or ripples on the back of the clubhead opposite the hitting area. The muscleback iron creates mass near the hitting zone, for additional power.

A: Modulus is a measure of stiffness. A high modulus shaft would have little flex while low modulus would be more whippy.

A: In the first half of the twentieth century, greens were kept much longer than the greens of today. In order to get the ball up and rolling on the green, the player had to hit a putt that would often resemble a chip shot of today.

A: The use of metals mixed into the golf ball's materials is said to strengthen the material to enable the ball to stay round and to recover from impact. Manufacturers also say that it enables them to help keep the ball balanced for better flight by distributing the weight of the metal throughout the ball.

A: Titanium is a very lightweight metal—it is often used in aircrafts because of this. When club manufacturers created irons made solely of titanium they had to make the clubhead very large, just to give it a swingweight that would be comfortable to most golfers. If they made the clubhead at normal size, the club would feel too light.

The Professionals

Q: What was the name of Tiger Wood's first PGA Tour victory?

Q: Tiger Woods won the NCAA and the National Amateur in one year. Who were the only other two players to accomplish this feat?

Q: What is Tiger's real first name, and where did he get the nickname Tiger?

Q: Why don't players on the professional tour concede holes or putts in sudden-death playoffs when the hole is obviously lost?

Q: Why do touring pros sometimes look into the cup while sizing up a putt?

A: 1996 Las Vegas Invitational.

A: Jack Nicklaus and Phil Mickelson.

A: Eldrick. His father nicknamed him after a Vietnamese
    soldier who was his friend.

A: Most of the PGA tournaments are medal play and require
    that all holes be completed. If a tournament goes into a
    playoff, it does not automatically become a match-play
    event.

A: They are not looking into the cup but at the rim around it.
    If the grass is clipped very closely on one side of the cup it
    may indicate that a putt will break in the opposite direction.
    As the mower passed over the cup it clipped the grass on
    the higher part more closely. Also, they inspect the rim to
    see if it has become broken or worn. If the rim is worn they
    may have to hit a putt that "dies" at the hole rather than a
    firm putt that might spin out.

Q: Why do many pros carry three wedges in their bags?

Q: Why do touring pros tend to walk by themselves in tournaments and not talk much with fellow competitors or the gallery during a round?

Q: Why do touring pros sometimes look straight up when they are selecting a club?

A: The third wedge added to the pitching and sand wedges is a club with an extremely high degree of loft, ranging up to about 65 degrees. This wedge is used for finesse shots of under 50 yards where the pro needs to pop the ball over a bunker or water and make it stop quickly. The club comes in handy as well for shots over trees, off hard pan and on steep downhill lies near the green. Many pros take the 3-iron out of the bag to make room for the third wedge.

A: It is not because they are unfriendly. The pros need to concentrate on the strategy required for the upcoming shot and do not want to become distracted. Secondly, under the Rules of Golf, they may not receive advice or assistance from anyone except their caddies. Should they accidentally discuss such things as club selection or course condition they may face a penalty. There are also penalties for slow play that each player must be aware of as he or she plays a round.

A: Some may be praying. Most likely, however, the pros are looking at the tops of the trees. The winds at the tree-top level will have a far more pronounced effect on their shots than the wind at ground level.

Q: Why do touring pros have to keep their own score?

Q: Why don't touring pros pick their own balls out of the cup after making a long putt?

Q: Why is the PGA Tour considered one of the most difficult major league sports to enter?

Q: Why do touring pros change balls every few holes?

A: The nature of the game demands that the "honor system" be used. In golf, the player himself may frequently be the only one aware of a rules infraction. For example, a player may be the only one to see any of the following infractions: a ball moves slightly after address; a new ball is put into play; a club is grounded slightly in a hazard; or a ball is struck twice during a swing. Most pros hold the integrity of the game in high regard and will call penalties on themselves without hesitation.

A: To avoid creating additional spike marks near the hole, the pros have their caddies, who usually wear sneakers, retrieve the ball from the hole.

A: To qualify for a spot on the PGA golfers must play well over a period of elimination rounds against the best players in the world. The players on tour who finish between 1 and 125 on the annual money list are exempt from qualifying. Players who finish 126 to 150 must qualify at a 108-hole tournament in December. For players seeking to break into the Tour, qualification begins in early fall with a 72-hole tournament followed by a second elimination tournament of 72 holes. The initial field of 1,750 is cut down to 155 players who join the twenty-five touring pros for the December tournament to select the fifty players who will receive tour cards for the coming year. The 108-hole tournament is a pressure-packed event where a bad hole might mean a year's plans down the drain.

A: Golf balls tend to get out of round after being hit several times. The pros change balls to prevent having to putt with a ball that is out of round and would not roll in a true manner.

Q: When sizing up a putt, why do touring pros often look at the edge of the green, even if their ball is nowhere near it?

Q: Why do pros on the tour often practice after their round?

Q: Why do touring pros dread wet conditions the most?

Q: Why do touring pros sometimes write something on their golf balls before playing?

Q: Why do touring pros count their clubs on the first tee?

A: The pros often look for places where water has run off the green. The flow of water from a green may assist them in judging slopes and breaks otherwise indiscernible.

A: Many pros say they practice after a round for two reasons— they played well or they played poorly.

A: The pros do not like wet conditions because reaction of the ball is unpredictable. The grooves on the irons become filled with water and reduce spin on the ball, which causes a knuckleball effect called a "flyer." This effect has the pros guessing at how far the ball will fly and how it will react upon hitting the green.

A: The pros are marking their balls for identification purposes. Because many pros use the same brand of golf balls, they place a few dots or circles on the ball to guard against mix-ups.

A: The Rules of Golf allow only fourteen clubs during play. The pros often swap clubs and try new clubs on the practice tee as they warm up for a round, and it is not uncommon for a stray club to wind up in a pro's bag accidentally.

Q: Why did the PGA Championship change from match to stroke play?

Q: Ben Hogan's first name is not really Ben. What is it?

Q: What pro has won the same tournament eight times?

Q: Who is the amateur who finished second in the Master's on two consecutive years?

Q: After graduating from Wake Forest, what career move did Arnold Palmer make?

Q: Why do the touring pros sometimes walk up to the flagstick, pull it out and then put it back in before making a chip shot?

A: In a word, television. A match play event is very difficult to follow in a television format, with some seventy-two pairings on the first day and the chance that the stars will not be available for action at air time. In a round-robin system, players are eliminated until there are only two left for the championship round. The championship takes place on Sunday afternoon, and the cameras have to follow only two players for over four hours. The PGA decided that in order to accommodate the television audience, a stroke event would be more entertaining and profitable.

A: William.

A: Sam Snead—The Greater Greensboro Open.

A: Charles Coe.

A: He joined the Coast Guard.

A: They want to ascertain if the pin is leaning in any direction. Sometimes a caddy will not place it all the way into the liner hole in the cup. When this happens the pin may lean against the player's line and keep a ball from dropping. The player may also be testing the rigidity of the pin. If the pin is very rigid, and the chip is makeable, the pro will probably remove the pin.

Q: Why is Al Geiberger called "Mr. 59"?

Q: During the 1986 British Open, this pro found out that his caddy was awaiting trial for murder. Who was this nervous star?

Q: In 1991, Lee Trevino switched from endorsing Toyota to endorsing what luxury car company?

Q: True or False? After winning the Grand Slam, Bobby Jones never won another tournament.

Q: Why do many touring pros stand directly behind the ball before taking their address?

Q: Who was the first man to win the U.S. Open who was neither American or British?

A: Al Geiberger has won ten PGA Tour events including the 1966 PGA Championship, but he will forever be known for shooting the lowest score in a PGA event to date, a 59 in the second round of the Danny Thomas Memphis Classic in 1977. Geiberger's business card opens to a replica of the Colonial Club's scoreboard and the hole-by-hole tally of his OUT 29-IN 30-59.

A: Gary Player.

A: Cadillac.

A: True. He retired.

A: The pros are sighting down the target line by lining up the ball with the spot where they want it to land. Many pick an intermediate target as well, a leaf, divot or discolored patch of grass a few feet in front of the ball and along the target line. When they take the address position they line up their feet, hips and shoulders along the line created by the ball and the intermediate target a few feet away.

A: Gary Player, in 1965, who hails from Johannesburg, South Africa.

Q: Who has won more U.S. Opens—Andy North or Arnold Palmer?

Q: Why do many PGA tournaments feature Pro-Am tournaments as a prelude to the actual event?

Q: What kind of grip does Tiger Woods use: Overlap, interlock, or ten-finger?

Q: Why are the pros on the bottom of a tournament scoreboard called the "dawn patrol"?

A: Andy North has won twice—1978 and 1985. Arnie's only win was 1960.

A: Money—the Pro-Am tournaments make up a large percentage of the prize money offered at each tournament. Entry fees for an amateur in these tournaments easily run into the $3,000-$5,000 range. Multiply that entry fee by 300 to 400 amateurs and the value of such events can be readily appreciated. Many corporations use the Pro-Ams as perks for deserving executives and enticements for prospective customers. There are long waiting lists for the chance to play in some of the more prestigious tourneys such as the Bob Hope Desert Classic or the Dinah Shore.

A: Tiger uses an interlocking grip.

A: The pairings for a tournament are done by score, with the leaders teeing off last on the final two days of the tournament. Thus, players at the bottom, or those who just made the cut, must tee off very early in the morning.

Q: Why is it said that "you drive for show but putt for dough"?

Q: Who is the only woman in LPGA history to shoot a 59?

Q: Who has played in the most Masters Tournaments?

Q: Why are the pros surveyed just before teeing off on the first and last days of a tournament?

A: It is felt that good putting is more important to winning money on the Tour.

A: Annika Sorenstam shot 59 at the 2001 Nabisco Championship.

A: Sam Snead—44.

A: The surveys are conducted by several independent market research companies who sell their information to the golf industry. Golf ball manufacturers, for example, use this information in their advertisements. Market research has shown that the golfing public, very conscious of the equipment and clothing used by the top professionals, make purchases (over a billion dollars a year) according to what is hot on the Tour. As an example, when Jack Nicklaus won the 1986 Masters using an oversized putter, McGregor was immediately overwhelmed with orders for it.

Q: Why don't the men pros wear shorts on very hot days?

Q: Why must an aspiring touring pro provide his financial statement to the PGA Tour before he is eligible to play?

Q: Why is the LPGA's Hall of Fame considered to be one of the toughest in all of sport?

A: The PGA Tour has strict guidelines for everything from abusive language to appearance. In the appearance category shorts are forbidden. It is felt that full-length golf pants are more in keeping with the Tour's image of gentlemen playing a gentleman's game.

A: The PGA wants to ensure that the pro has the financial ability to stay on the tour for the year. PGA officials do not want no-shows or open slots at a tournament because a pro could not afford the trip.

A: The LPGA Hall of Fame has exacting criteria for admittance compared to the election format used in other sports. To be admitted to the LPGA Hall of Fame, a woman has to win thirty victories on the tour, including two different majors; thirty-five victories with one major; or forty victories without a win in a major.

Q: Why do some touring pros have their caddies read their putts?

Q: What father and son won PGA tournaments on the same day?

Q: Who was Arnold Palmer's caddie during his heyday?

Q: Why do many pros insist that their caddies carry the golf balls in their pockets?

Q: Why do some professionals take a semi-backswing just before they make their actual swing?

A: Most touring pros read their putts alone. Some have their caddies give their opinions on the speed and break, and others use their caddies as sounding boards, explaining the putt as they think out loud.

A: David and Bob Duval. On March 28, 1999 David Duval won the Players Championship only one hour after his father Bob Duval won the Emerald Coast Classic.

A: "Iron Man" Avery.

A: This practice is called "warming the eggs." Many pros believe that warming the golf balls help them to fly farther. While warming does enhance the elasticity of the ball, it would require illegal means to raise the temperature of the ball to get any significant benefits from it.

A: Players such as Justin Leonard and Tiger Woods often take a semi-backswing just prior to the actual swing to rehearse the swing plane of their backswing. This little move helps them to take the club back in a path that is not too inside or too outside of their intended backswing. The waggle lets them feel the proper takeaway path.

Q: Why do some caddies tip the pin backward while tending it for their player on tour?

Q: Why are some professionals chipping with fairway woods?

Q: Why do professionals always seem not to know the Rules and ask for a rules official when they have a question?

Q: Why don't professionals take a practice putt after they hole during a tournament as they do in the Ryder Cup matches?

A: Caddies often tip the pin backward from the hole because it gives the player a sense of the line to the hole. With the pin tilted backward, it looks like a line being extended beyond the hole to the player.

A: Several professionals have begun chipping with fairway woods under certain conditions. If the ball is on a thin lie, having little grass underneath it, or on a course rough around the green, then the pros may use the fairway wood. It avoids the chance of hitting behind the ball, or fat. The wood tends to glide on the ground, gets the ball moving with a slight bump into the air, and then rolls onto the ground.

A: It is not that they do not know the Rules of Golf as much as it is avoiding the possibility of being disqualified. For example, if a player has to take a drop and if for some reason his drop is not within the Rules, knowingly or unknowingly, a fellow competitor or official who witnessed it may question it after the round. Then, he/she may be disqualified and ineligible to win. By having a rules official present, the player gets a stamp of approval right on the spot.

A: The Rules of Golf prohibit practicing on the course during medal or stroke play. Thus, taking a putt over after finishing a hole would be a two stroke penalty. In match play, such as in the Ryder Cup, "practice" on the course is allowed under the Rules. In this format, players often re-play a putt to get the feel of a green or see why they missed a putt after they have holed out.

The Course

Q: Why is it said that "putts always break toward the water"?

Q: Why is "The Country Club" of Brookline so named?

Q: On what famous course does the "valley of sin" protect the 18th green?

Q: Two of the holes at St. Andrews are named after golfers. Who are they?

Q: Why do many golf courses in Japan have two greens per hole?

A: It is not that the water has some magnetic force on the ball. Water, of course, seeks its lowest level, which is usually a body of water—an ocean, lake or pond near the green. As water drains toward the body of water it tends to shape the slope toward the direction of the pond or lake. Additionally, the grain on the green tends to grow in the direction of a water source. These factors cause a putt to break in the direction of a body of water.

A: The site of the 1988 U.S. Open has been referred to as The Country Club since its beginning. It was built as a "park where members may be free from the annoyances of horse railroads and meet for pleasure, driving and riding." The club was formally established in 1882. The Country Club gained fame when a young Francis Ouimet won the 1913 U.S. Open in a playoff against Harry Vardon and Ted Ray.

A: St. Andrews Scotland.

A: Bobby Jones (10th) and Tom Morris (18th).

A: The Japanese climate has extreme ranges in temperature. Bent grass, the preferred grass for greens, tends to burn out quickly in the hot, humid summers. To solve this problem, the Japanese decided to build two greens per hole. One green would have bent grass, which would be regrown each year. The other green would be of korai, a very tough grass imported from Korea which can withstand harsh winters. Thus, Japanese clubs offer their members two greens, one for summer and one for winter.

Q: Why is the famous Olympic Course in San Francisco called "the course that was built in reverse"?

Q: Why are there "dogleg" holes?

Q: Why are there so many tee locations and so much teeing space at most courses?

A: In 1922 the Olympic Club, a private social club, purchased a course near Lake Merced called Lakeside. The course was located on the bare side of a large hill that ran down to the lake. The Olympic Club immediately began planting eucalyptus, pine, and cypress trees to outline each of the eighteen holes. The trees matured some twenty-five years later to become an essential part of the challenge and beauty of Olympic. That trees were planted on an existing course rather than having holes carved out from a forest gave birth to the expression "built in reverse."

A: Dogleg holes were first designed about seventy years ago to break the monotony of straightaway holes and afford the golf architect some leeway in matching design characteristics and golfing skills. The dogleg hole may tempt the long hitter to cut over trees or water to gain a closer approach shot.

A: The amount and location of teeing ground determine the leeway architect and greenskeeper have when planning shotmaking and maintenance. Nine-hole courses often have significant differences in the tee-markers from front to back nine to bring variety and afford players the challenge of hitting different shots on the same hole. In championship conditions, the tee locations may be used to add distance and increase the level of difficulty of a hole. To set a course record, a competitor must use the back tees.

Q: Are all flagsticks the same height?

Q: Why is the stretch between the eleventh and thirteenth holes at Augusta National called "Amen Corner"?

Q: What president of the United States had a putting green installed behind the White House?

Q: Why is one trap at Oakmont called "Church Pews"?

A: The USGA recommends that the flagstick be a minimum of seven feet high. Manufacturers generally adhere to this size because of perspective. If flagsticks varied in height from course to course it would be difficult to judge distance.

A: The origin of the term "Amen Corner" is credited to Herbert Warren Wind who noted that if you can negotiate these three holes in par a prayer is in order. The three holes have had a long history in deciding the Masters.

A: Dwight Eisenhower.

A: Between the third and fourth holes at Oakmont there is a trap that is 60 yards long that is set to catch stray drives from both holes. The trap has seven grassy ridges that run across it giving the appearance of church pews.

Q: Why is the fourth hole at Baltusrol famous in golfing lore?

Q: Why is Pine Valley often considered the top golf course in the United States?

Q: Why is the eighteenth tee at Harbour Town called "Nicklaus tee"?

A: Baltusrol hired the famous golf architect Robert Trent Jones to toughen up the course for the 1954 U.S. Open. After he finished his task by making alterations on several holes, the members complained that he had made the course too tough. The new fourth hole, for example, required a tee shot of almost 200 yards across water to a well-bunkered par 3. Jones, along with the club pro, club president and the chairman of the Open committee, actually played the fourth hole to rate its toughness for themselves. After the first three had hit their shots, Jones teed up and holed out the shot for an ace. He simply shrugged: "As you can see, gentlemen, this hole is not too tough."

A: Pine Valley, located in Clementon, New Jersey, places a premium on accuracy and distance that few courses can match. Many of the holes at Pine Valley do not have continuous fairways but rather narrow and demanding landing areas. Stray shots do not land in simple rough: sandy scrub brush and water abound along the landing areas. The par 3s demand that the ball land and hold the green, and the par 5s average around 600 yards and require three perfect golf shots to get home.

A: Harbour Town Golf Links, located on Hilton Head Island in South Carolina, is the site of the Heritage Golf Classic. The eighteenth hole has several tees, but one is located in a position that requires a drive of 250 yards to a peninsula portion of the fairway. Many Harbour Town members say it would take one of Jack's drives just to reach the fairway.

Q: Why do greenskeepers use the term "put to bed" in regard to a golf course?

Q: Why is the sand trap on the seventh hole at Pine Valley called "Hell's Half-acre"?

Q: Why is the famous golf course Baltusrol so named?

A: Greenskeepers in the north "put the course to bed" in late
     fall. The procedure usually entails covering the greens to
     prevent damage from frost and ice, placing snow fences
     around greens and tees to prevent skiers or snowmobiles
     from cutting tracks into the turf, and digging special
     drainage ditches for traps or particularly wet spots along the
     course. The purpose, of course, is to survive the winter in
     good shape and be ready for an early opening in the spring.

A: The seventh hole at Pine Valley has been called the most
     exacting par 5 in the world. Its 585-yard length is not the
     real problem: the huge expanse of sand and scrub brush that
     begins 285 yards off the tee and extends for over 100 yards
     creates one of the most challenging holes in the game. The
     giant sand trap that defines this golf hole is in the *Guinness
     Book of World Records* as the world's largest sand trap and is
     affectionately known as "Hell's Half-acre."

A: Located in Springfield, New Jersey, Baltusrol's name is
     derived from a farmer of Dutch origin named Baltus Roll,
     who once owned the land.

Q: Why are those new, very short courses called "Cayman" courses?

Q: Why does the ball seem to sit up better on the fairways of Florida courses?

Q: Why is the sixteenth hole at Firestone called "The Monster"?

A: Cayman courses, which run around 4,000 yards in length, were first put into use in the Cayman Islands. Special balls that travel a shorter distance than normal are used to play these courses. The first Cayman courses were developed in the early 1980s.

A: Most of the courses in Florida use Bermuda grass, a wiry, coarse-bladed grass that grows well in warm climates. Because Bermuda grass is so thick, it holds the ball up on the fairway much more effectively than grasses such as Poa annua or bent.

A: The sixteenth at Firestone is a 625-yard par 5. While downhill, the advantage of the slope is negated by the lie usually left for the long second shot home. Water guards the green in front, prohibiting even the boldest player from firing at the green from a distant, downhill lie. Legend has it that only two players have ever hit the green in two in competition—Firestone's club pro and former PGA Champion Bobby Nichols and Arnold Palmer who used the word "monster" to describe the hole after he took a triple-bogey 8 on it in the 1960 PGA Championship.

Q: When holes are rated for strokes, why are some difficult holes rated lower than holes that seem easier?

Q: Why is Oakmont famous for its sand traps?

Q: Why are some courses called "stadium" courses?

A: Difficulty is not necessarily the main criterion in deciding
     which holes are to be considered the stroke holes in an
     order from one to eighteen. The USGA's guidelines call for
     consideration to be given to a poorer player in a match
     against a superior player, so that the main criterion is the
     place where the player needs the stroke most. Also, the
     stroke holes are distributed equally on the front and back
     nines (odd-numbered on the front, even-numbered stroke
     holes on the back). Though the holes on one nine may be
     tougher than on the other, the stroke holes still must be
     distributed equally. Generally holes are graded in the
     following order: difficult par 5s, difficult par 4s, remaining
     par 5s, remaining par 4s and par 3s. Of course, exceptions
     may be made for especially tough par 3s and 4s.

A: Oakmont opened in 1904 with an incredible 350 bunkers,
     almost twenty per hole. In order to cut maintenance costs
     the number was gradually cut to 171.

A: Stadium courses are specifically designed to accommodate
     large galleries for PGA Tour events. Many of the older
     courses on the tour are surrounded by trees or water that
     prohibit galleries from getting a good view of the golf
     action. Stadium courses are designed with large slopes
     around the greens, viewing perches, walking paths and
     other facilities to facilitate large groups of golf fans and
     offer them a better view of play.

Q: Why do some courses have wicker baskets instead of flags on their flagsticks?

Q: Why are some courses called "executive" courses?

Q: Why is Wack-Wack, a course on the Asian Tour, so named?

Q: Why is the famous Golden Horseshoe course in Old Williamstown, Virginia, so named?

Q: Why is the 10th hole at Carnoustie in Scotland called "South America"?

A: Originally flagsticks were just plain staffs. Eventually they sported small disks with the number of the hole on them. Most flagsticks at the turn of the century were about three feet tall. The Sunningdale Course in England used wicker baskets to help golfers see the pin placement better from any angle. The wicker-basket pins were also very popular in England because they did not aid the golfer in determining the strength and direction of the wind.

A: Because executive courses are shorter than championship courses, they can be played more quickly, and the busy executive can get a round into his schedule.

A: Often the site of the Philippines Open, Wack-Wack Golf and Country Club is located near Manila. It got its name from the sound of crows, which were extremely numerous and bothersome to the players in the early days of the course.

A: In 1716, the governor of Virginia, Alexander Spotswood, led an expedition from Williamsburg over the Appalachians and back. Upon returning to Williamsburg, he gave each member of the expedition a golden horseshoe.

A: Legend has it that near the turn of the century a young, local player who had hopes of making his fortune in South America as a golf pro, played a farewell round at Carnoustie. Having celebrated with Scotch before and during the round, he passed out on the 10th hole. The Scots said that is as far as he got.

Q: Why is the large tree in front of the tee on the seventeenth hole at Augusta called "The Eisenhower Tree"?

Q: Since St. Andrews was the site of the beginnings of organized golf, why isn't the Royal and Ancient Golf Club of St. Andrews considered the oldest golf club in the world?

Q: Why is there a World War I memorial placed near the 12th green on Turnberry in Scotland?

A: President Eisenhower loved to play at Augusta National, but the large tree on the left side of the fairway became his personal nemesis. Ike used to hit a slice and would always aim down the left side of a fairway. On Augusta's 17th, his ball seemed to end up in the tree every time.

A: The Royal and Ancient is not the oldest golf club in the world. The Honorable Company of Edinburgh was established in 1744. Thus, the Honourable Company was in business ten years before the Royal and Ancient.

A: The land of Turnberry has particular sentimental value for those who fought in World Wars I and II. The course was turned into an airfield in both wars. The evidence of the airstrip can be seen along the 12th hole, and a memorial to the war dead of World War I was erected on a hill near the green.

The Rules

Q: Why are there fourteen clubs?

Q: Why do players drop a ball at an arm's length rather than over their shoulder as they used to do?

Q: Joe's ball lands in a trap and is nestled against a dead squirrel. Can he remove the squirrel under the rules?

Q: Why is there a rule against grounding a club in a sand trap?

Q: Why is there a rule against "building a stance"?

A: Theoretically, if there were no limit to the number of clubs a player could have a club for every possible contingency and thus have an unfair advantage over the competition. The USGA and the Royal and Ancient agreed on fourteen because it represented a standard set of clubs—2- through 9-irons, a wedge, a putter and four woods.

A: The modification in the Rules had several intents. While dropping a ball for relief, a player would often bounce it off of his shoulder or heel by accident, so that the ball landed outside the drop area. The drop over the shoulder also often caused players to toss the ball rather than drop it. By extending one's arm for the drop, the likelihood of the ball remaining in the intended drop area is increased.

A: No. The squirrel is a loose impediment.

A: Rule 13-4 prohibits the touching of soil, sand, or any living thing in a hazard as a means of preventing testing the texture and thereby gaining an unfair advantage. A hazard is considered a form of punishment for a stray shot. Testing the sand or soil would partially negate the effect of the "punishment."

A: If there were not a rule against building a stance a player could take measures that would certainly be unfair. For example, a golfer faced with a downhill lie could use a small pedestal or fill in the ground to make his stance level. Players could also use devices to help them push off their back foot. The rule is intended to make everyone play the course as intended.

Q: What is the diameter of a hole?

Q: Why does Rule 10 state that players who play out of turn in stroke play will be disqualified if their intent was to give an advantage to a player?

Q: Why do the Rules of Golf place so much emphasis on amateur and professional status?

Q: Eddie is in a deep greenside bunker and cannot see the flagstick. He asks his partner, Joe, to hold the stick up in the air while he plays the shot. Is this legal?

Q: Why can't a player go to an adjoining sand trap, take a swing to test the consistency of the sand, then step into the trap in which his ball lies and play it?

A: 4.25 inches.

A: The rule is intended to prevent two or three players agreeing to hit first in order to help someone. The scenario might go as follows: Two players are hopelessly out of the hunt in a stroke tournament. Their good friend Bob is only a few shots back with five holes to go. As a favor for their friend, they agree to hit before Bob. Bob is able to see what clubs were hit, how the ball travels in a wind condition and how it reacts upon landing. This type of behavior would be a serious breach of the Rules and a common sense of fairness and deservedly carries the penalty of disqualification for those involved.

A: The Rules of Golf have almost ten pages on the status of amateur and professional. The main emphasis is on fairness. It would not be fair for someone who derives his living from the game to play against those who play golf as an avocation. Much of the attention the Rules give to status is the definition of what constitutes being a professional and how one may apply for reinstatement as an amateur.

A: Yes.

A: This practice would not be in keeping with the spirit of the game and is prohibited by the Rules. Rule 13-4a states that "a player shall not . . . test the condition of a hazard or similar hazard."

Q: If your ball lands in casual water in the rough, can you drop the ball on the fairway if that is the nearest point of relief?

Q: Why is there a rule against using foreign materials on a golf ball?

Q: Why do some scorecards have a figure called "slope" on them?

Q: Why are pin placements made as they are in tournaments?

A: Yes.

A: Rule 5-2 was written with the intention of preventing a player from gaining an unfair advantage by using a substance that could change the flight characteristics of the ball. For example, a ball sprayed with a slippery substance does not have as much sidespin, so that hooks and slices can be avoided. Such actions, not dependent on golfing skill, are outlawed.

A: Handicaps may vary from course to course, depending on length and difficulty. Every player should have a USGA handicap expressed in strokes and a fraction of a stroke as well as the handicap that he carries at his home course. If a player travels to a new course he or she may convert the USGA handicap into a course handicap by using the Course Handicap Table on the scorecard or posted in the clubhouse which is known as the "slope."

A: There are no specific rules in regard to the location of pins. Greenskeepers, however, use some general guidelines of fairness and common sense in cutting the holes. At most PGA tournaments the holes are usually cut six on the left, six on the right and six in the middle so as not to favor players who prefer to draw or fade their shots into the green.

Q: Why are tournament officials concerned with time in golf?

Q: Why can't a caddie hold an umbrella over his player while he putts?

Q: Why can you move a hazard stake that interferes with your swing when you cannot remove an out-of-bounds stake in a similar situation?

A: The Rules of Golf mention time several times. Although advocates of the game love the lack of a clock, in tournament golf time comes into play: a ball is lost if it is not found within five minutes; failure to start on time may result in disqualification (though if the player arrives within five minutes he may be penalized two strokes in stroke play or lose the first hole in match play); and finally there are penalties (two strokes in stroke play, loss of hole in match play) for undue delay on the course.

A: Rule 14-2 (assistance) states: "In making a stroke, a player shall not accept physical assistance or protection from the elements." The rule is intended to prevent one player who has special equipment or help over someone who does not.

A: A hazard stake is an obstruction. Whether it is movable or not depends on how it is installed. Objects defining out-of-bounds are not obstructions and cannot be removed.

Q: Why are the rules-making meetings called "quadrennial conferences"?

Q: Why is a stroke counted for a player who swings and misses the ball because the wind blew it off the tee before the clubhead arrived?

Q: Why don't the touring pros use binoculars to survey the area for their shots?

Q: Why do the Rules allow practice on the course before a match play event but not stroke play?

A: The Rules of Golf are formulated in a joint effort between the Royal and Ancient Golf Club of St. Andrews and the United States Golf Association. Delegates from the two associations meet twice a year to review proposed changes. The rule book, however, is published only every four years, thus the name "quadrennial" is affixed to the conferences.

A: Rule 11-2 states that a ball may be re-teed if it falls off the tee while addressing it. However, once a player makes a stroke—"a forward movement of the club made with the intention of fairly striking at and moving the ball"—it is indeed counted.

A: Rule 14-3 prohibits artificial devices and unusual equipment. Such items as range-finders and survey equipment would greatly take away from the spirit of the game and give too much prominence to technology over golfing skill.

A: According to Tom Meeks, director of Rules and Competitions for the USGA, there are no specific reasons why you can practice in the one case but not in the other. In fact, the note at the end of Rule 7-1 permits the Committee to reverse this rule. Mr. Meeks goes on to explain that the main reason why practice is permitted in match play is that there are only two players. In stroke play the numbers would be so large that practicing on the course could be a big administrative problem, and the maintenance crew might not be able to complete its work.

Q: Why is so much emphasis placed on club design in the Rules of Golf?

Q: Why do many pros hold their clubs out of the grass in the rough as they address the ball?

Q: Why was croquet-style putting outlawed?

A: Five very specific pages in the Rules of Golf detail the permissible design of clubs in order to keep the game one of skill rather than one of technology. The flight characteristics of a golf ball can be greatly influenced by such design modifications as the width between grooves on an iron, the mass of the clubhead, flex characteristics of a shaft and the material of an insert into the clubface. The basic idea is to preserve the game of golf as a function of a player's skill and not the result of advanced technology.

A: It is legal to ground your club anywhere on the course except in a hazard. However, if the ball moves after you have taken your address, there is a one-shot penalty. To address the ball under the Rules you must 1) take your stance and 2) ground the club. Many top players hold the clubhead a few inches from the ball so that technically they have not addressed the ball. Should the ball move in this situation, there is no penalty.

A: Rule 16-1e prohibits standing astride or on the line of a putt. Croquet-style putting enjoyed a brief period of popularity when Sam Snead used it to cure his "yips." The croquet style, however, was never a traditional golf stroke, and never considered a fair stroke. Additionally, a player would gain a distinct advantage by being able to sight directly down the line of a putt as compared to the traditional manner of putting. Rule 16-1e was put into effect to preserve the traditional and inherent fairness of the game.

Q: Why do most players feel it is difficult to play to their assigned handicap?

Q: Why can't players tamp down spike marks on the green?

Q: Why was it that, in the original Rules of Golf, there was one that stated, "You must tee your ball on the ground"?

A: The USGA's system for computing a handicap does not measure the player's actual scoring average but rather his/her potential. The handicap is based on the last 20 rounds played but only the lowest 10 are taken for use in computing one's handicap.

A: There have been several explanations for this Rule. Firstly, tamping down spike marks might allow a player to get an advantage by creating a small "path" along his or her line while pressing down the marks. Another reason is that with numerous spike marks, the pace of play at all levels would be slowed down greatly as players tamped down all marks along their lines. More and more players, including the professional tour players, are using spikeless shoes that eliminate spike marks altogether and make the greens smooth for everyone.

A: This rule seems to have been made to prevent golfers from using bushes or shrubs and making a baseball-like swing. This type of teeing the ball was said to be used by Germans playing the game *Kloven*.